VALLEY 1/2
5069001057
LeBoutillier, Nate.
The story of the Golden State Warriors /

VALLEY COMMUNITY LIBRARY
739 RIVER STREET
PECKVILLE, PA 18452
(570) 489-1765
www.lclshome.org

CREATIVE EDUCATION

Published by Creative Education
123 South Broad Street
Mankato, Minnesota 56001
Creative Education is an imprint of The Creative Company.

DESIGN AND PRODUCTION BY **EVANSDAY DESIGN**

PHOTOGRAPHS BY Getty Images (Andrew Bernstein / NBAE, Bruce Bennet Studios, Focus on Sport, Otto Greule Jr. / NBAE, Walter Ioos Jr. / NBAE, Jed Jacobsohn, Michael K. Nichols / National Geographic, NBA Photo Library / NBAE, Rich Piling / NBAE, Jeff Reinking / NBAE, Wen Roberts / NBAE, David Sherman / NBAE, Ernest Sisto, Jon Soohoo / NBAE, Rocky Widner / NBAE)

Copyright © 2007 Creative Education.
International copyright reserved in all countries.
No part of this book may be reproduced in any form
without written permission from the publisher.
Printed in the United States of America

LIBRARY OF CONGRESS CATALOGING-IN-PUBLICATION DATA

LeBoutillier, Nate.
The story of the Golden State Warriors / by Nate LeBoutillier.
p. cm. — (The NBA—a history of hoops)
Includes index.
ISBN-13: 978-1-58341-407-1
1. Golden State Warriors (Basketball team)—History—
Juvenile literature. I. Title II. Series.

GV885.52.G64L43 2006
796.323'64'0979461—dc22   2005051202

First edition

9 8 7 6 5 4 3 2 1

COVER PHOTO: *Baron Davis*

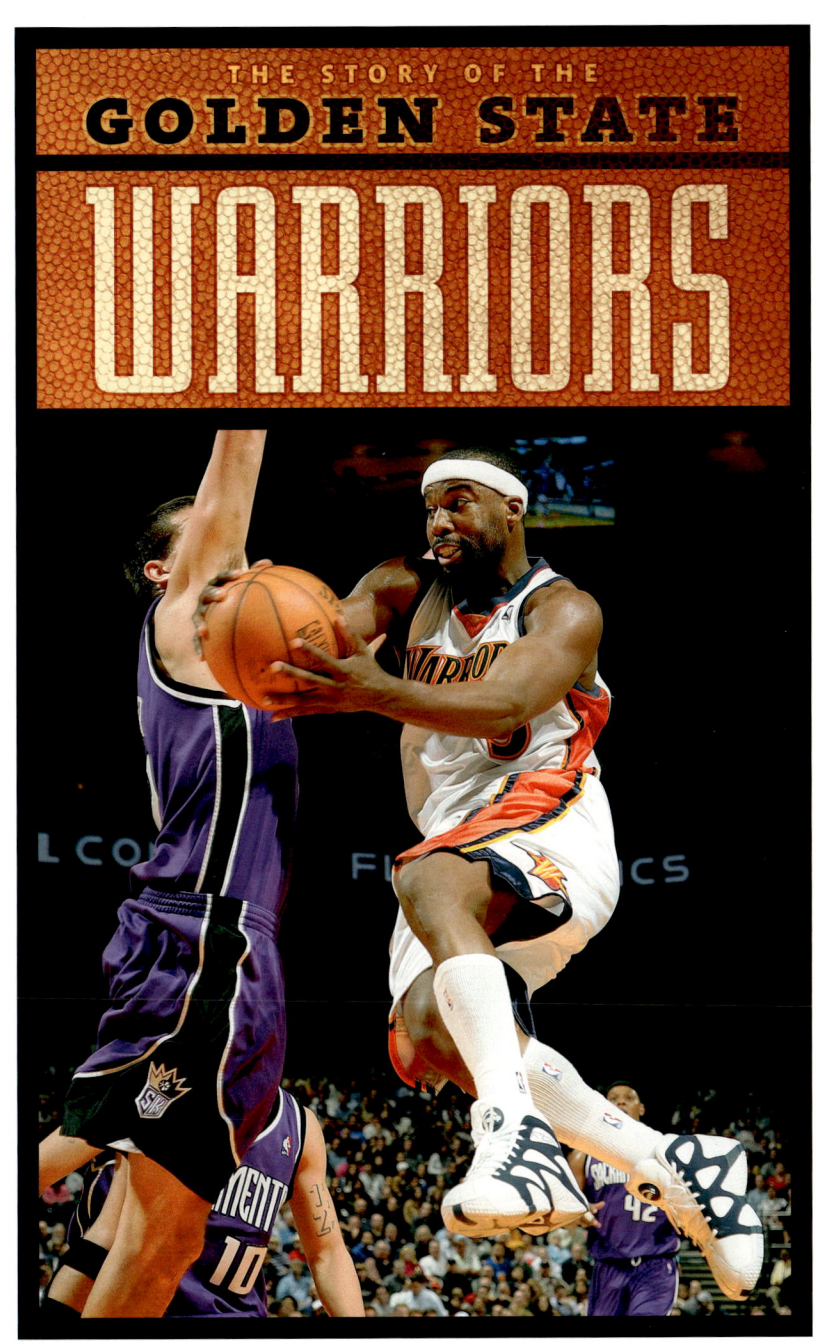

THE STORY OF THE GOLDEN STATE WARRIORS

NATE LeBOUTILLIER

CREATIVE EDUCATION

Five against five.

Dribble the ball. Pass the ball. Shoot the ball into the basket. Basketball can be the simplest of games. Every so often in team sports, a lesson is repeated, and that lesson is: keep it simple. The 1974–75 Golden State Warriors re-taught that lesson to the rest of the National Basketball Association (NBA). Sure, the team had talented individual players such as Rick Barry and Jamaal Wilkes. But these Warriors played simple basketball as a team, trusted in each other, and were rewarded with the highest honor in basketball: an NBA championship.

FROM COAST TO COAST

THE BAY AREA OF CALIFORNIA IS MADE UP OF TWO neighboring cities: Oakland and San Francisco. The cities are about three miles apart, separated by the San Francisco Bay. Although the two Bay Area cities have always competed in some respects, they also share a common interest—a team in the NBA. Although this franchise, known as the Golden State Warriors, started out in Philadelphia, Pennsylvania, the team has called the Bay Area home since 1962.

GOLDEN STATE

WARRIORS

The Warriors have always been a coastal franchise, beginning in Philadelphia and ending in California

9

Much of the Philadelphia Warriors' early history was written by Paul Arizin (left) and Joe Fulks (right)

When the first major professional basketball league—the Basketball Association of America (BAA)—was formed in 1946, one of its charter teams was the Warriors of Philadelphia. The team's founder and first coach was basketball pioneer Edward Gottlieb. Gottlieb began building by signing a high-scoring forward from Kentucky named Joe Fulks, who led the league in scoring in 1946–47 with 23 points per game. "He made one-handed shots, jump shots, right-handed [and] left-handed set shots from a distance, driving shots, hooks with his right or left hand," said Gottlieb. "He was also basketball's first jump shooter."

Led by Fulks, the Warriors won the first BAA championship in 1947. The BAA and another league merged to form the NBA in 1949, but by 1952–53, the Warriors dropped to 12–57. Two new arrivals, guard Paul Arizin and center Neil Johnston, then helped Fulks take the team back to the top. Philadelphia leapt to a 45–27 record in 1955–56, then captured its first NBA championship, beating the Fort Wayne Pistons four games to one before record crowds, including a high of 11,698 fans at Philadelphia's Convention Hall for Game 3. NBA basketball seemed to be taking off.

THE "GRANNY" SHOT

Young basketball players not yet strong enough to shoot baskets normally often resort to flinging the ball at the hoop underhanded, or "granny" style. It looks a little silly, but for two Warrior greats, granny was golden when it came to shooting free throws. Wilt Chamberlain tried shooting grannies (and other styles), but he made only 51 percent of the free throws he attempted in his career. But Rick Barry was another case. The Hall of Fame guard was a 90 percent career free-thrower using the granny style. "My dad kept on me that I could be better if I shot underhanded," Barry said. "I tried it basically to make him stop bugging me. But when I went out and worked with him, little by little I realized that, 'Hey, this isn't too bad.'"

WILT THE WARRIOR

IN 1959, THE WARRIORS MADE 7-FOOT-1 AND 250-pound Philadelphia native Wilt Chamberlain their "territorial" selection in the NBA Draft. Sportswriters dubbed him "Wilt the Stilt," but Chamberlain preferred to be called "The Big Dipper"—a name he garnered because of the way he would often have to dip his head under doorframes when entering a room. "He could do whatever he wanted to do on a basketball court," Warriors coach Frank McGuire said. "No player, not even Bill Russell, could stop him."

Bill Russell, the great center for the Boston Celtics, couldn't exactly stop Chamberlain, but the Celtics won 9 of the 10 NBA championships in the 1960s, and Russell led the way. During those years, Chamberlain and Russell challenged each other in quite possibly the NBA's greatest ever matchup at the center position, but the Celtics continued to top the Warriors.

Basketball legend Wilt Chamberlain led the NBA in both scoring and rebounding in his first four seasons

HOOPS

Nicknamed "The Destroyer," hard-nosed guard Al Attles gave the Warriors 11 seasons of fierce defense

With attendance in Philadelphia waning, Gottlieb sold the Warriors in 1962 to a group of San Franciscan investors, and the Warriors headed west. Chamberlain continued to dominate, leading the NBA in scoring for the fourth straight year, but the Warriors finished a mere 31–49 in 1962–63.

In 1963, Alex Hannum was hired as coach. Hannum knew his team had talent; Guy Rodgers and Al Attles formed a solid backcourt, and young forward Nate Thurmond played a big role as a rebounder and shot blocker. But the coach depended mainly on his star center. "For us to win," Hannum explained, "Wilt has to play like Bill Russell when we're on defense and play like Wilt Chamberlain when we're on offense."

Hannum guided the Warriors to the 1964 NBA Finals, but they fell to the mighty Celtics. After San Francisco got off to a poor start the next season, the Warriors, wanting to develop a more team-oriented attack, traded Chamberlain back to Philadelphia, where a new pro team—the 76ers—had cropped up. For all his great years with the Warriors, Chamberlain failed to bring the franchise a championship trophy.

WILT'S BIG NIGHT

Early in his pro career, Wilt Chamberlain scored points for his hometown Philadelphia Warriors like no one had ever seen. But on March 2, 1962, in Hershey, Pennsylvania, before 4,124 fans, Chamberlain outdid himself, scoring an astonishing 100 points in a 169–147 victory over the New York Knicks. In the game, Chamberlain made 36 of 63 field goals and 28 of 32 free throws. When he scored the 100th point with 46 seconds remaining, fans swarmed the court to congratulate him. "It was my greatest game," said the Warriors center. "It's a record I'd hate to try to break myself." Although Chamberlain averaged an NBA-record 50.4 points per game over the 1961–62 season, his archrival, Bill Russell, won the Most Valuable Player (MVP) award, and Russell's Celtics won the NBA title.

GOLDEN STATE'S QUEST FOR GOLD

THE CHAMBERLAIN TRADE ALLOWED TWO NEW Warriors stars to rise. The first was Thurmond, who quickly evolved into one of the NBA's best centers. The other was young forward Rick Barry, who joined the Warriors as a frail-looking youngster in 1965. Over the next few seasons, Barry proved capable of scoring almost at will from anywhere on the court, and his deadly shooting earned him the nickname "The Golden Gunner."

In 1966–67, Barry led the NBA in scoring with 35 points per game, and the Warriors again reached the Finals. There they faced off against the 76ers, led by their old teammate Chamberlain. Barry poured in an average of 41 points per game in the Finals, but Chamberlain and the 76ers prevailed in six games.

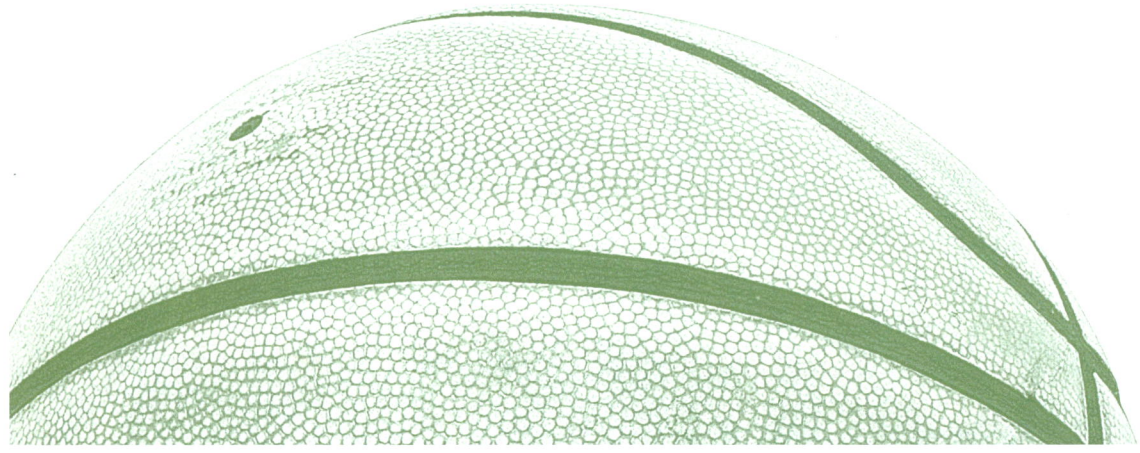

GOLDEN STATE WARRIORS

Sharpshooting guard Jeff Mullins hit 84 percent of his free throws in 1968–69, second-best in the NBA

HOOPS

NBA

Rick Barry's incredible shooting skill and fiery competitiveness made him a legendary scoring machine

The next season, Barry left to join a team in the new American Basketball Association (ABA), and Thurmond was injured. Without their stars, the Warriors struggled, and longtime Warriors guard Al Attles took over as head coach. Another major change soon followed. Since arriving in the Bay Area, the team had played home games in three different cities—San Francisco, Oakland, and San Jose. Finally, in 1971, the team settled in the Oakland Coliseum Arena and became the Golden State Warriors.

Once resettled, Attles focused on his lineup. Thurmond anchored the inside, while guard Jeff Mullins led the Warriors in scoring. In 1972, Rick Barry also returned to town. The Warriors of the early '70s were successful in the regular season, but failures in the playoffs. The 1974–75 season changed all that. Before the season, Thurmond was traded to Chicago for center Clifford Ray. The Warriors then added guards Charles Johnson and Butch Beard and rookie forward Jamaal Wilkes to the starting lineup. With a fast-break offense and a gambling defense, the Warriors soared to a 48–34 record.

The Warriors then headed into the 1975 playoffs with determination. In the playoffs' first two rounds, the Warriors toppled the Seattle SuperSonics and Chicago Bulls to reach the NBA Finals. The Warriors faced the heavily favored Washington Bullets, but in a stunning upset, the Warriors swept the series in four straight games to win the championship. "We cared about winning and did whatever we could to win," said Barry. "It was an atmosphere you'd like to see more professional teams have. I defy anyone to find anything like it."

Like Rick Barry, Chris Mullin was a rangy forward with the ability to score from anywhere on the court

TOUGH TIMES BY THE BAY

THE NEXT SEASON, BARRY, WILKES, AND SWINGMAN Phil Smith powered the Warriors to a 59–23 record—an all-time franchise best. But the team failed to repeat as champs, falling to Phoenix in the playoffs. That playoff loss signaled the start of a gradual decline for Golden State. Despite the best efforts of such players as sweet-shooting forward Bernard King and immovable center Joe Barry Carroll, the team missed the playoffs every year from 1977–78 to 1985–86.

In 1988–89, Coach Don Nelson took control in Golden State, developing a wide-open offensive attack that revolved around the team's sharpshooters, forward Chris Mullin and young guard Mitch Richmond. In 1989, the Warriors drafted point guard Tim Hardaway. The team continued to improve and played an exciting, high-scoring style that kept fans riveted. In 1990–91, the Warriors won a playoff series, but lost in the second round. The next year, the Warriors traded Richmond away and lost in the first round.

GOLDEN STATE WARRIORS

Rare quickness made Tim Hardaway an All-Star equally skilled at scoring, passing, and playing defense

23

A bruiser with a soft shooting touch, Chris Webber was the first overall pick in the 1993 NBA Draft

In the 1992 NBA Draft, the Warriors drafted forward Latrell Sprewell. "Spree," as he was known to Golden State fans, never seemed to tire on the court as he flew from end to end. In his second season, Sprewell teamed up with Hardaway and talented rookie forward Chris Webber to lead the Warriors to a 50–32 record and a playoff berth.

Unfortunately, just when it looked like Golden State was approaching a championship, things fell apart. The coaches and players feuded, and in 1995, Webber was traded to the Washington Bullets, and Nelson stepped down. Hardaway was soon traded away as well. By the end of the 1994–95 season, the Warriors were 26–56.

In 1997, the Warriors brought in new head coach P.J. Carlesimo, but an incident early in the 1997–98 season derailed the Warriors' progress. During a practice, Sprewell and Carlesimo got into an argument, and the All-Star guard physically attacked the coach. Sprewell never played for the Warriors again, drawing a one-year suspension from the NBA before being traded.

RUN TMC

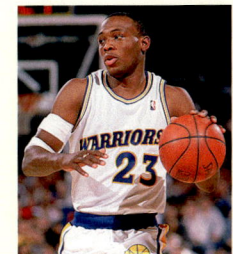

As the 1980s gave way to the 1990s, one of the coolest rap music groups was a New York City trio known as Run DMC. At about the same time, the Golden State Warriors were one of the most fashionable teams in the NBA because of their own trio, Run TMC. The letters "T-M-C" stood for Tim, Mitch, and Chris—Tim Hardaway, Mitch Richmond, and Chris Mullin. Let loose to "run 'n' gun" (fast-break and shoot at will) by coach Don Nelson, Run TMC thrilled fans with high-scoring shootouts in an often sold-out Oakland Coliseum. In 1990–91, all three players averaged more than 20 points per game in leading the team to a 44–38 record and a first-round playoff series win over the San Antonio Spurs.

RETRO COOL UNIFORMS

With more than 50 years under its belt, the NBA has seen fashions come and go. Since the year 2000, the NBA has embraced "retro" uniforms—an updated fit of an old style. The Warriors' "The City" uniforms were introduced for the first time in 1962 and worn again in 2004–05. The simple blue-and-gold jerseys with the Golden Gate Bridge and the words *The City* on the front debuted against the Knicks in New York. Warriors players were nervous about showcasing their new threads in "*The City*," but Big Apple fans appreciated them. Said guard Al Attles, "Nobody wanted to be the first to take the [warm-up] jacket off. Finally, we take the jackets off and I'll be darned if we don't get a standing ovation from the New York crowd."

One of the fastest players in basketball, forward Latrell Sprewell spent six seasons with the Warriors

WARRIORS TODAY

THE WARRIORS STRUGGLED AFTER THE SPREWELL incident, missing the playoffs in each of the next seven seasons. Players and coaches were shuffled like cards in and out of the franchise as the team sought to assemble a winning combination.

But in 2001, things finally started looking up. Athletic guard Jason Richardson and bruising forward Troy Murphy both joined the Warriors via the NBA Draft, and the next year, forward Mike Dunleavy was selected. These three players formed a foundation in Golden State, avoiding the trades that had so often whisked the Warriors' best players away.

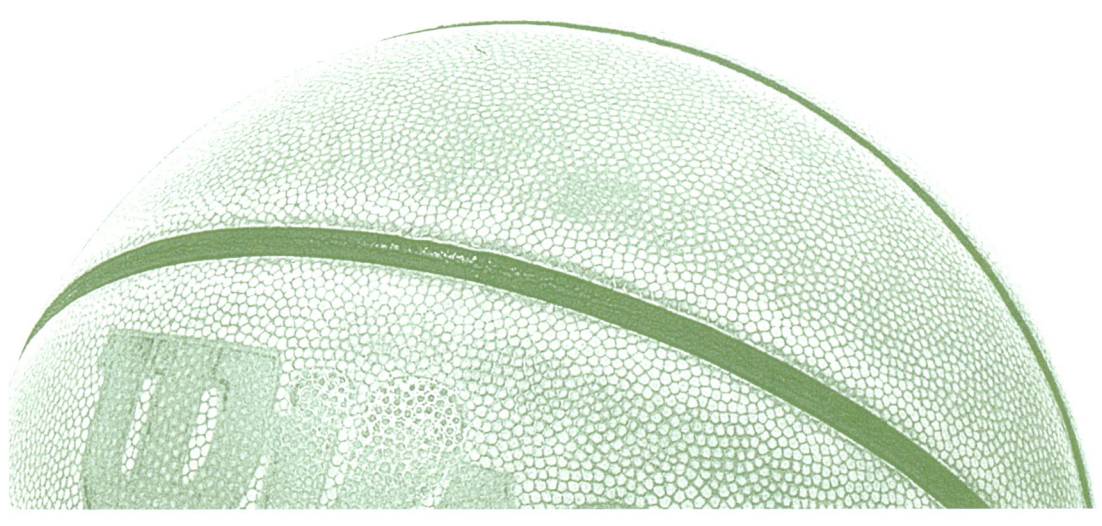

Mike Dunleavy played college ball at powerhouse Duke University before suiting up for Golden State

A tough defender, gifted passer, and surprisingly strong rebounder, Baron Davis could do it all.

During the 2004–05 season, the Warriors made a trade for Baron Davis, a high-flying point guard previously with the New Orleans Hornets. The Warriors missed the playoffs again, but with Davis, they caught fire over the season's final 18 games, going 14–4. "The thing I love about Baron is he delivers the ball on time," said new head coach Mike Montgomery. "You don't have to wait, you don't have to reach, the ball is delivered on time and it's delivered to you. He's a true point guard."

With a solid nucleus of players in place, Warriors fans hope Golden State will soon recapture the impressive team play that led to two NBA titles. The game can be simple, and Golden State has a great blueprint from its past to study and try to implement. Today's crew of Warriors plans to soon bring another golden trophy to Golden State.

JASON RICHARDSON, SLAM DUNK CHAMP

The "slam dunk" has become the most popular shot in basketball. So when Warriors guard Jason Richardson won the NBA Slam Dunk Contest in both 2002 and 2003, he saw his own popularity rise. The judges for the 2003 contest were all former dunking champions, including Michael Jordan. For his best dunk, Richardson tossed the ball in the air and caught the bounce while going into his leap. With his back to the rim, he passed the ball through his legs with his right hand and dunked over his head with his left hand. "It's an honor to be only the second player to win it back-to-back," Richardson said. "I know Michael was the only guy to do it. To have him as one of the judges up there, it was a dream come true."

INDEX

A
American Basketball Association 19
Arizin, Paul **10**, 11
Attles, Al **14**, 15, 19, 26

B
Barry, Rick ("The Golden Gunner") 5, 11, **11**, 16, **18**, 19
Basketball Association of America 11
    championship 11
Beard, Butch 19

C
Carlesimo, P.J. 25
Carroll, Joe Barry 22
Chamberlain, Wilt ("The Big Dipper") 11, 12, **13**, 15, **15**, 16
Convention Hall 11

D
Davis, Baron **30**, 31
Dunleavy, Mike 28, **29**

F
Fulks, Joe **10**, 11

G
Golden State Warriors
    first season 11
    relocation 15
    uniforms 26
Gottlieb, Edward 11, 15

H
Hannum, Alex 15
Hardaway, Tim 22, **23**, 25

J
Johnson, Charles 19
Johnston, Neil 11

K
King, Bernard 22

M
McGuire, Frank 12
Montgomery, Mike 31
Mullin, Chris **20-21**, 22, 25
Mullins, Jeff **17**, 19
Murphy, Troy 28

N
NBA championships 5, 11, 19, 31
NBA Finals 15, 16, 19
NBA playoffs 11, 15, 16, 19, 22, 25
NBA records 15
NBA Slam Dunk Contest 31
Nelson, Don 22, 25

O
Oakland, California 8, 19
Oakland Coliseum Arena 19, 25

P
Philadelphia, Pennsylvania 8, 11, 12

R
Ray, Clifford 19
Richardson, Jason 28, 31, **31**
Richmond, Mitch 22, 25, **25**
Rodgers, Guy 15
Run TMC 25

S
San Francisco, California 8, 15, 19
San Jose, California 19
Smith, Phil 22
Sprewell, Latrell ("Spree") 25, **26-27**, 28

T
Thurmond, Nate 15, 16, 19

W
Webber, Chris **24**, 25
Wilkes, Jamaal 5, 19, 22